First Kiss on Mars

Stephen Jenkins

Cover photography by RODNAE Productions

1: First Kiss on Mars (2022)

Night Ride
Pwll y Glaw
The Whale
Light Pollution
The Long Cold Waking
Sleep all day; out all night
The First Kiss on Mars
Bokeh
The Club
Pagan Song
Fortune & Glory
Just
In the Margins
Doorstep
March
Waterwords
Old Dogs
Starlings Under the Eaves
Better Days
In Bloom
House of Wax
Fledgling
Counselling
At the Strangest Times

2: Adverse Camber (2009)

Hands (I)
Hands (II)
Shoe Gazing
Historic Battles
The Other Woman
Salvage
Not Fade Away
Chang'e
Skyscraper
Sea Legs
Superpowers
The Artiste
Grandmother
Bedtime Sonata
From Life
Autumn

3.Named for Gods (2014)

The Mobile Galaxy
My Fair Lady
Walking on the Spot
Martha Vickers
Our Love
Apparition
Named For Gods
Dwarfed
Impact Theory
Eveningstar

First Kiss on Mars
(2022)

Night Ride

Night ride, with Jupiter on your left; Saturn
faint and lost to the clouds. The lights
are silver solder in the dark. We drive
circuits along the motherboard until
we idle at a junction and drown our
thoughts in the static of the radio.
Sliding into first, we don't see how it
works. But I'd slip the cap and lift the catch
and light a fire under your hood. We'd
lie side-by-side, parallel with cat's eyes.
And I wish it was morning so we could
glide past friends taking breakfast. You'd wave
and smile as we rolled by. Windows down,
your hair blowing. Everyone seeing. Everyone knowing.

Pwll y Glaw

It's a row of houses near the viaduct, we walked
through from Richard Burton's house. You
showed me where a pub used to be. They all

claimed to be his local. They were all probably
right. The gutters filled with rain and drains
gurgled. We kissed in the car park. It didn't
feel like our last; my hands in your back

pockets. You shook your hair from your eyes
and smiled. *Wear me in the lull before pushing
on through the doldrums*. And in my mind:
clear skies and days upon the sea. In yours: what
you'd leave; memories and silver thread to find
upon my sleeves.

The Whale

Her song fuels the lan-
terns; her bones in bod-
ices. 19th Century
plastic. Meat on the
plate. Pulled from the waves.
The whaler dies too
from a cancer borne
by sin from the sea-
songs he silenced with
his rusted harpoon.
Or maybe it was
the tobacco. There'll
be no flensing of
his fat, his meat will
rot and bones become
dust; or his body
will be spread: ash on
the wind.

Light Pollution

I wish we were pins so we could wear each other
out. You should write lists; fill up your journal

for rain-soaked days. Add in
a wish. I'd bottle up the night sky for when
the stars are outshone by lights from a car

dealership. There's not a moment of darkness
in this town. When I think of you I realise that
distance is the greatest

aphrodisiac. What celestial sexual tension hides
behind clouds? And you could make me come

to your house under any pretense you'd like. I'd
sing words to soar through your door; slip through
your ribs. Lock them in your chest, until they seep
through to your bones to be pushed past lips.
Nothing outshines a melody.

The Long Cold Waking

Morning layers sirens over city's
hum traffic horn section pedestrian
thrum spin on the wind stepping
on cracks she smokes a cigarette
next to an old tree's bark
    in winter's bite
and last night she felt the train
humming stepping on tracks the whisper
of the engine as it passed like a coven
of ghosts late and rushing and rushing
and late in and gone like a middle eight
she dances through gardens jumping
gates and fences stepping on cracks
and the walls that have crumbled
tripping on roots broken through
the ground they outgrew and in
    the shattered
glass strewn through the grass
she sees a hundred of her
and a hundred promises

Sleep all day; out all night

held in my cupped hands
orb of dust and rock we wrapped
men in steel and threw them
across the dark

and on the regolith I put
my boots and plastic
men in airtight suits
and a flag in army green

and on a cloudless night I'd gift
you a giant leap and banish
to you the monsters that creep
behind the black of my bedroom door

and when it rained a wish
a kiss unanswered
I'd bury a list in your craters
never shared never found

and on tranquility base I'd place
a glow that warms through outer-space
far from earth a mother's
embrace always felt always seen

The First Kiss on Mars

Only we would hear the tink of our helmets
touching. Our faces scrunched, lips puckered,
leaning, reaching, gloves too thick for the feeling.
An almost embrace for two souls encased, we
flutter inside separate cages. Later, we'll stow
our suits: unlaced like Victorian corsets. The walls
around us would rattle from dust and wind.
Nobody knocking, no one to let in. We'd roll under
Agency-issued sheets, skin to skin; the connection
complete, and bring life to a dead planet.

Bokeh

Do you remember those plastic cylinders, like
small black pill jars? It seemed there were
always a couple in a drawer somewhere. They'd
rattle with memories, never to be opened because
they'd die in the light like what's inside a chrysalis
or pupa. How many still sit in drawers, attic boxes
or landfills? Evocations that never got the chance
to react to chemistry, to spread colours across
paper gloss. Moments captured, undeveloped
and as good as lost.

The Club

[It was] one of those, miles-from-anywhere places, you'd have to taxi or walk it. Then you'd queue to the muffled pulse of a bass line and the rush of loudness when the main door opened like a DJ pushing up sliders on a mixing desk. It was a tease. You wanted to be inside that sound.

There'd always be girls so glamorous sucking the night air through clenched teeth. The queue would move, roused from slumber to shuffle a small way towards the door. The girls would be stamping high-heeled feet. Fuck, it's cold. Arms wrapped in coats, but legs bare to the wind's bite. Later, their kisses would taste of coconut and pineapple.

You'd all be giddy to get in or maybe from your mate's cider that gets passed around. The next day you'd remember the lights and the music, if you were lucky. Never the queue, never the walk home. You'd always be dancing not staggering, laughing not freezing, your voice torn and raw from shouting. And at breakfast you'd chat, was alright, yeah. But in your thoughts you're already back there striding through the cigarette smoke past the threshold, the whoosh of the sound holds you, pulls you together. Today and every day, it's Friday night, forever.

Pagan Song

Clean fields
                        roll
                           away from
                                         the vista
                                                    like green waves
along a
                        sea
frozen in time
            You could stand there
alone and howl
                                               into the sky
It's a pagan song
and once it's sung
you can never go home
               there will always be a part
of you
               screaming
               into the wind
lungs raw

this is Wales
              valleys
terraced houses
and the mines
                   that gave my grandfather
work and
              emphysema
lungs raw
                                          and
they still say
                        the mines gave
the Welsh a living
                              but really
                              it was a dying

Fortune & Glory

Hands strike
under bright
lights and it's not like
when you've practiced
it alone. Catching air.
A full room, crisp and
deafening. Someone
whistles, and the guy
who came second
follows you right into
the bathroom to shake
your hand. If it's any
consolation: it's fleeting.

Just

You don't need to be afraid
to express what you feel
to a man paid to think

he understands the deeper
things that can hide between lines

and can name the meter
and gets the rhymes and line
breaks it's okay just to love
the sounds that words make

In the Margins

Closed eyes close to other
worlds clear sky clouded
thoughts bewitched by

moonlight in the moments
before morning of not quite
dreaming that blur the lines

between the dead and
the sleeping you were still
here breathing and when

you were alive I never
noticed the rise
and fall of your chest

but your vessel was still
in the chapel of rest

not a sound
not a breath

Doorstep

You're the ever flowing
water that resolves
into the turning tide
you're the sapphire horizon
I'm a sea bird calling

calling

I try not
to stop outside
your window but my reflection
beckons me

I close my eyes
so tight the red lids go
black and I can imagine
it's a mirror and this
is a future yet to be

we're like a record
of pristine vinyl
I'm the favourite song
you've yet to hear how
I long to push your door
and sing out your name
so clear

and past the threshold
up your hall long and wide
to your room where you don't know
you've been waiting
your eyes as green
as the light at a crossing
and everything becomes mine

March
(after Dali)

I know you're sleeping
the wind rattles the letterbox
and whooshes against the windows

you can't see the clouds but if you could
you know they'd be moving fast across
the night sky and I'd walk it step after step
single file up mountain sides down the valley

and i know you're sleeping
but it's been too long since i pushed one arm
            under your neck and the other around
your waist pressed close my skin cold
and wet from the weather my insides hot
from the exercise step after step

you float on your pillow
                                                feathers whisper
in your dreams asleep in this world
awake in another maybe
you are walking
too

Waterwords

Sometimes you spill
an inkwell and mop
at its sides knowing
that you can't get it
back into glass
but you can make
it more pleasing
a stain
            or maybe
it's picking to rain
and you are catching drops
in a tea cup all the while
wishing it was a wall
not water and you could
go at it with a lump hammer
and bolster because words
fail and become blocked

but liquid can't be stopped
it'll always find its way to a page
and a reader sat backlit
no distractions
fingers and thoughts
ready to explore

in their hands they hold you
in dead wood and imagination

Old Dogs

Weekend workshops among
anthologies of poets
old men as rusted
as the library's rails
read their work
into their printouts
and only in their minds
mock your awkward
rhymes and they're glad
you came

with teabags and they
all know they're the best
in the room and two hours
are over too soon or not
soon enough and as you pack
up your papers and stuff
they'll say they're glad
you came

with teabags
and a pound for the tin
with a handshake and a smile
down stairs and out
past shelves and shelves of
shelf-worn dust covers rows
rows rows of paper parcels
worlds in words in stasis
never to be unpacked again

Starlings Under the Eaves

Clutch hatched and hungry
          chorus
like five phones ringing at once
          answer
a relay of worms
          back garden bullies
chasing off sparrows that dare to dirt bath
          too near
but they have their own problems
          bickering in the blackthorn
to the ground floats tree and bird leaf

and I found in the soil a small skull
          hollow and absent of song
but the skies sing with spring
          warnings and messages

Better Days

It's a quiet day save the wind
and the flutter of wings to the bird table.
Chat heads are marble stones
mourning the death of check-ins,
friendships, or small talk.

The only message chime comes from inside,
like a siren cutting through silence:
Reminders of the voice behind the static smile,
a name on the cusp of a breath.

But the siren swells, and the heart beats
louder than thoughts, and the distance
between my thumb and you becomes

a span too far to bridge,
too great to negotiate. Words on the tip

of my tongue freeze

at the tip

of my fingers.

In Bloom

It's still dark, but the sky is warmed by a waking
sun just below the horizon. The air is filled with
song. Not light enough to forage, songbirds give
the morning a melody, voices carry; marking their
territory.

Blossoms in full bloom line a train track, pinks
and whites ready for release. At the station sits a lone
girl in the fluorescent glare of a vending machine,
her thoughts busy like the electrical hum.

She waits for the familiar clack of wheels upon
tracks and the weightless glide of a five thousand
ton engine. It's coming and for a moment she
holds her arms out in a cross, ready for the breeze
to grip and hold her aloft.

But the air is still save a morning chill and
the train's whisper and hiss. She's safe in its belly
as it heaves into a float. Her ticket is one way,
and in the rumble and sway, spring blossoms
blow away.

House of Wax

Town's like a house of wax.
    Girls with glazed faces jerk
forward in heels too high, drawn
    to the smell of chips fried in days-old
oil and it would only take a slip or trip
    to upend a candle stick and set fire
to the night like a Vincent Price mansion.
    Why is opulence always so flammable?

Town's ablaze with vaping teens and queues
    between kebab shops and Kentucky
and a vampire couldn't float past those pale
    young throats. From the curbside
shuffle Dracula's would-be brides. He seeks virgins
    but a chicken doner will have to do.

Town's awash with rain and the wax girls
    and vamps huddle under canopies
and brollies as mad doctor Frankenstein laughs
    into the night sky. His monster tries to pull his
shock-haired mate into a taxi. She screams.
    But weren't they made for each other?

And the undead and insane head to their beds
    ...or someone else's with rolling heads
or drunken kisses.

Spending Saturday nights hammered.

Fledgling

two weeks old
you hopped around
my patio small enough

to fit in my hand
wings unable
to carry you upwards like

your siblings you ruffled
and puffed your grey down
but no one came so you

found a corner away
from the commotion
of the bird feeder sat

silent and slipped onto
your side
my hands found you shivering

then still
the other sparrows returned
to feast at the table

you got the same
as them
a beginning and an end

and as I placed you in the hole I'd dug
your eyes reflected the sky

Counselling

It ain't working but you wonder
what it would take to scrub

the rust from cogs so they would
propel you smiling into tomorrow
days punctuated by laughter
only cry at a birthday surprise

eyes wide and

all it would cost is a lien on your dreams
a plasterboard partition in your aspirations

road closed
lights off

you'll make it work even if you have to
cradle every stillborn possibility

At the Strangest Times

Friday found me crying
over chocolate coins
in Morrison's. You find me
at the strangest times;
pulling a collage of Christmas
mornings to memory.

I can't
push the pieces
into the slots. Your absence
is a puzzle I can't solve,
and I'm working through
the novelty of talking to you still,
and getting no change.

Adverse Camber
(2009)

Hands (I)

She shows me signs
with hands
soft as any whisper

She says that in her mind
my voice
is as beautiful as the lines I sing

And without listening
she hears
every word I say

Hands (II)

I'll wash them just one more time.
Through the lather of the soap
I can see the filth on my hands.
I scrub harder as the water gurgles down the sink
and I glance out the window and I think:
I'll wash them just one more time.

Shoe Gazing

Running over crisp crunching
ground, games with friends
in hooded sweatshirts. We speed
past the breath we leave hanging
despite bruised shins and aching

bones. She's sitting, shivering
under a tree, arms crossed.
I join her with stutters,
my eyes buried in her trainers, laces
tied like my tongue. She must think

I have a thing for shoes. They
are all I have the courage to look at.

Historic Battles

From across a desk,
Mr Jones swooped in.
Finger and thumb goggles,
with elbows as wings.
Was he a Spitfire?
Were we Messerschmitts?
Over the English Channel,
we'd be blown to bits.
How disappointing in sixth form,
to know the man,
quiet and calm.
With warm handshakes,
and "call me John".

The Other Woman

The raindrops
upon her roof
are fingertips
tap tap tapping keys;
typing pages
of insincerity.
She slumbers
inside my elbow,
oblivious
to her role
in this fiction.

In silence
we drove to the tip.
Your car filled with broken
tools of domesticity.
Did I see a little
smile on the lips
that he kissed,
as we carried
boxes from the boot?
Once empty, we headed
to our homes,
leaving behind
what we couldn't
salvage.

Not Fade Away

The air; your house.
You drift in waves
that roll to drums
and down canals

to the soul. The brave
invite you to a new
magnetic home. A shell
on a shelf. They revel

in your release
again and again.

Chang'e

if he squinted he could
see that pretty teen
who sang and danced
and once had been
the girl life whirled
around

now lines and lies circle
her smiles but the eyes
still flash with youthful
surprise at the kiss
that had once been
a wish on a long list

lips brush
and the soft hush
is broken
as she giggles
into his mouth

another woman twice his age
mother would be so disappointed

Skyscraper

That old oak
was like a
phone, every ring
told a story. We
climbed and branches
snapped like staples
binding Friday's
reports. I was King
Kong. You: Fay Wray.
And, if they ask,
I'll still say I fell
swatting bi-planes.

Sea Legs

The boys laugh as the old drunk sways
from starboard to port.
"Come on you old fucker, crack a smile!"
And he smiles a jig-jig jigsaw,
steadying his sea legs to take another swig,
but spills himself
across the pavement.
Moments of white noise,
before he hoists his head,
heaves his shape
from the floor, swearing.
The boys roar, secretly hoping,
after the lines and creases come,
they won't end up that drunk.

Superpowers

Of what use are friends
to a refugee from a dying galaxy?
His repulsor rays can clear rooms;
his invisibility lets him slip into the night sky.
Unnoticed.
Yet every night,
he fills a glove with warm water, entwines
the fingers with his own
and imagines the feeling
you earthlings call "love".

The Artiste

She puts her hand
over my crossed fingers
and breathes in my kiss
and my lies; all performed with open eyes.
The dull ache of attachment
throbs in my teeth.
Love is like an industrial acid;
not for consumption.

Grandmother

"I'd rather feed you for a week,
than a fortnight,"
a barely audible
echo of words
I've never heard
from a woman I've never met.
As friendly as nettles,
the queen of cross words
hunched over a bucket
of coal, an image
not quite a picture,
not like the familiar
monochrome photograph
of her
smiling.

Bedtime Sonata

Your cheek scratches
the pillow
as your jaw
creaks and clicks.
You're picking out bass lines
of medium wave radio songs
the ceiling robs
of treble.
Only their rumbling bedrock
is determined enough to seep
through the boards.
Then, It's gone,
and your heart stamps
as regular as infantry
marching to a symphony
of white noise.

From Life

I breathe and eyes
fix on thighs
and twist
into my murdered Madonna.
The pose that pleases.
Boys that shift,
red-faced flatter,
brushes paint a me
too idealised to offend.
I prefer older
men, harder
poses pay more. They understand
the difficult
truth on the page.
It's hard being
bohemian
on the living wage.

Autumn

When I was seven
my teacher ripped
up my colouring
I kept going
out of lines
Carrot orange Crayola
bled too far into beaver brown
Now raw sienna sets
over umber branches
not quite bare
from fall
and when I squint
they all go
out of lines

Named for Gods
(2014)

The Mobile Galaxy

From the forefinger of Patrick Moore hangs
celestial bodies of gas and rock
strung with elastic: the solar system.
No room for insignificant forms;
Phobos and Deimos, dead moons of mars,
Pluto and Eris too small to be worlds
in the Scattered Disc too far to picture.
Prod Venus, so pretty, pearly and white
so they spin round their polystyrene Sun.
Always in motion, they lull me to sleep.

My Fair Lady

Moon mirror ripple
shakes the calm.
Never seen her
smile,
let alone wink.
Yet through watery
illusion she blinks
and sways
and seems
more alive
than the girl
who scowls and sighs
when I sneak
a hand
over her eyes.
"Guess who?"

Walking on the Spot

The girls don't
love the swirl the caramel
clouds and whipped cream
that tease across your jelly bean
surface yet boys forget
the enormity of distance
and time and lives
fade like a daydream
too easily lost
when you awake
with a start
water
through
your
fingers
grass
through
your
toes

the brightest star in the September sky

failed sun
god of gods

Martha Vickers

Don't go to Venus
our prettier twin
She's a femme fatale
a Lauren Bacall
planets don't care
for telescopes
Mars is not concerned at all
with inquisitive eyes
that focus on a wry
Bogart smile of dust
on terracotta plains
a wink a hint
of something more
hidden
beneath fedora skies

Our Love

Our love,
like Triton,
spins the other way.
The moon, a pretty
pearl doomed, her orbit
decays towards Neptune's
embrace. Even titans
are transient and all breakups leave scars.

Our love,
like Triton
will spread dust and light
into rings so splendored
they'll rival even Saturn's.

Apparition

With the naked eye:
Fastest brightest redd-
ish largest farthest.
Wander among them.
Galileo dared.
What of those unseen?
Giants revealed
through mathematics.
Celestial dreams
dreamt through glass eyes
and equations.
Distance. Numbers. Light.

Named for Gods

The colossal, the insignificant
All jostle for position
Amidst crimson showers
Above the swirling torment
Of mother's embrace.
Having 62 moons isn't like
Having 62 kids,
And Saturn doesn't look
A day over eternal.

Dwarfed

Toffee apple? Candy floss?
Nothing can appease
the sunken shoulders
and pronounced pout
of poor little Pluto.
Too short
to ride the "I'm a
Real Planet" rollercoaster.

Impact Theory

They think (or thought)
our world and an object
Mars-sized did collide
and create a child
that would curate
the tides. Yet millimetre
by millimetre plots
to leave the Earth
behind. The way
all children do.

Evening Star

Mercury
in the west
setting soon
after the sun
mankind evanescent
the Earth
an eventide
home but dreams
are unfailing never
fading retaining
vigour
fresh
in leaf throughout
forever

www.ingramcontent.com/pod-product-compliance
Lightning Source LLC
LaVergne TN
LVHW040957150826
845672LV00002B/733

* 9 7 9 8 3 5 6 1 8 0 3 2 3 *